Cosmic Rituals

An Astrological Guide to Wellness, Self-care and Positive Thinking

ALISON DAVIES

Illustrations by Eleanor Hardiman

Hardie Grant

QUADRILLE

Live Your Best Life

Look up into the sky on a clear night and you'll see the stars shining. Arranged in an array of glorious constellations, they can't help but unleash their brightness. The ancient Babylonians were the first to chart the path of the Sun by splitting it into the twelve signs of the zodiac, but early civilizations have always looked to the stars for inspiration. The patterns and characters formed became players in the night sky and, like any roles, they developed attributes and traits which were associated with each sign.

Whether you're a luscious Leo or a lovely Libran depends on where the sun was in relation to the Earth on the day you were born. Astrologers believe that this dictates the personality traits and talents you are gifted with. The positions of the planets have other influences, too, affecting your physical appearance and the way you think and feel. Knowing and understanding these strengths can help you harness this power for peace of mind and wellbeing so that you can truly make your mark in the world.

There's no one-size-fits-all when it comes to taking care of yourself, but your star sign provides a blueprint for you to work with. Working to your personality type can help you find the best self-care plan for you, one that complements your astro superpowers.

If you're a fan of all things cosmic, a regular star-sign reader or just mildly interested, this book gives the lowdown on how you can live your best life, based on your zodiac sign. There's everything from hints and tips on wellness, herbal healing and de-stressing to mindful moments and techniques to make you feel energized and ready for anything.

When you follow the trends suggested by your astrological make-up, you work to your strengths and nurture your needs. But don't be limited by your own zodiac energy. There are many different planets in your chart that affect your personality and you can use their energy too. Look at page 127, which shows you the primary energy of each zodiac sign, and see how you can broaden your rituals to capture other zodiac energies. So if sensitive Cancer is looking to feel more grounded, head for Capricorn's rituals, or if bold Leo has been roaring a little too loudly, then Libra may be able to help.

Do what feels right for you and have fun. There really is no better way to find your sparkle than by looking to the stars!

Aries

21 March–19 April

Element
Fire

Planet
Mars

Aries Stars
Lady Gaga (28 March)
Heath Ledger (4 April)
Billie Holiday (7 April)

Mantra
'I find moments of
stillness in every day.'

The Essence of Aries

Armed, ready and raring to go! Time is precious to Aries, especially when you have a goal in mind. You're a fire sign, and that means you're passionate and motivated: drive has never been a problem. You're not afraid to take responsibility and stand up for what you think is right, which makes you a good leader, while your sunny personality makes you a popular friend. You have your moments, though. You find it frustrating when things don't go to plan or when others can't keep up. But you need to admit that being forced to slow down actually gives you a much-needed boost. Get the balance right and the world is your oyster!

Your Self-care Plan

Your rituals and techniques work to your strengths and fit naturally into your daily routines. You need the energy to stay as a front runner, as well as techniques to get you back on track when you've run too far, too fast. Finding that balance is essential for this first zodiac sign.

Morning Ritual to Get Up and Glow

• Stand barefoot and drop your weight into your knees.

• Feel your soles connect with the floor and picture tiny roots growing from each foot. Imagine them sinking beneath the ground, anchoring you to the Earth.

• You feel strong, stable and relaxed.

• Lunge as low as is comfortable, then push yourself up into a standing position.

• Take a deep breath and draw in energy from the Earth.

Crystal Prescription

On-the-go rams never have enough hours in the day. While you enjoy the buzz, slowing down and finding some inner calm will help you see the bigger picture and achieve more in your day. Taking time out and using crystals with a loving, uplifting energy will help you gain the patience you lack, feel more relaxed and build empathy.

Amethyst

The calming energy of this stone stills a swirling mind and cuts through clutter, making it perfect for those wanting to be more intuitive.

Keep a piece at work, or in your home office, to promote peace and clarity of mind.

Angelite

A stone with a light and gentle energy, angelite promotes compassion to help you connect with others on a deeper level.

Soften your heart by holding the angelite over the middle of your chest for a few minutes each day.

Daily Stress Busters

Monday
Let go of pent-up energy by jumping on the spot or doing star jumps for a minute.

Tuesday
Cuddle your pet to turn a frown upside down, lower the heart rate and boost your happy hormones. No pet? Walk your neighbour's dog, or cat-sit for a friend.

Wednesday
Slow down your breathing by counting the length of each breath and adding an extra beat. Do this for a couple of minutes to feel relaxed, then energized.

Thursday
Put on your favourite song and sing along at the top of your voice and pour all your frustration into each note.

Friday
Tell your nearest and dearest how much they mean to you to feel instantly brighter.

Saturday
Thank the universe for five things that you are grateful for.

Sunday
Eat mindfully, savouring each mouthful, and visualize the food nourishing your body.

Self-love Ritual

You always expect the best, especially from yourself, but a little self-kindness is also important.

• Curl up in your favourite chair where you won't be disturbed and wrap yourself in a snuggly blanket.

• Close your eyes and picture yourself cocooned in cotton wool.

• Imagine you're circled in a loving embrace. Relax your chest and nestle into the softness.

• For even deeper relaxation, add a few drops of lavender essential oil to the blanket and inhale the aroma.

Daily Balancing Meditation

Picture yourself floating on the ocean, your arms and legs cushioned by the waves. The water is warm and comforting and gentle ripples brush against your skin. The surface sparkles under the sunlight and you feel safe in the ocean's serene embrace. In the distance, you can see a golden stretch of empty beach. You are completely alone, undisturbed and enjoying the stillness. This is a place of wonder where you can simply be. It doesn't matter where you are or where you are going. In this moment, right now, you are exactly where you need to be. There is no need to do anything except breathe and enjoy the experience. Close your eyes and let yourself drift on the current.

Boosting Basil for Aries

A member of the mint family, aromatic basil has anti-fungal and antibacterial properties. Associated with the planet Mars, it's the ideal herb for Aries, helping to boost the mood, enliven the senses and cleanse mind and spirit.

To make a basil hair rinse, steep a handful of basil leaves in a pan of boiling water for around 30 minutes. Strain into a jug (pitcher), then leave to cool. Pour over your hair and massage into your scalp before the final rinse. The combined scent and massage will help you to generate new ideas.

Mindful Moment of Action

Taking time out doesn't come naturally to you, so be mindful while you are on the move.

Walking to work or taking a stroll? Use the time to engage your senses. Really look at your surroundings, notice the shape and structure of things, the colours and the way they blend. Pick up on those little noises you usually miss. Listen to your breathing and how it fits in with the other sounds around you; notice the sound of your feet and the rhythm of your walk. Breathe through your nose and pay attention to faint aromas in the air around you. Notice the taste of the air and how it feels to really focus on your breathing.

A Good Night's Sleep

As an active ram, sleep isn't high on your list of priorities and you get away with as little as possible. But quality sleep will keep you firing on all cylinders, so learn to wind down properly before bed.

• Give technology a break. Switch off your devices at least an hour before bed.

• Soak in a relaxing bath with a few drops of lavender essential oil to help your body unwind.

• Keep your bedroom well aired to lower your body temperature and help you nod off.

Taurus

20 April–20 May

Element
Earth

Planet
Venus

Taurus Stars
William Shakespeare (23 April)
Audrey Hepburn (4 May)
Adele (5 May)

Mantra
'I express myself with
confidence and ease.'

The Essence of Taurus

Tenacious Taurus – while you might underestimate your talents, the world sees a different picture. Shouting about your achievements doesn't come naturally to you, but with your creative flair and charisma, you will always be noticed. Caring for others is a big part of who you are, and you can be extremely tolerant, to the point where it's no longer any good for you. The flip side is that when you're pushed, you will eventually go off like a rocket. Bottling up anger makes a bull feel blue, but your nearest and dearest are the perfect antidote, along with some much-needed me-time to banish stress. When you're firing on all cylinders, nothing can stop you.

Your Self-care Plan

Your plan concentrates on releasing stress so that you remain positive and focused. You tend to hold on to emotions and let them fester, so rituals that help you express yourself and your creativity are empowering. These exercises heighten your strengths and abilities while promoting inner peace. Building self-esteem will give you the confidence to turn your dreams into reality.

Morning Ritual to Get Up and Glow

• Salute the sun by throwing back your curtains to let in the light.

• Place your feet firmly on the floor and crouch down into a ball.

• Breathe in deeply and slowly unfurl until you're standing with your arms pointing to the ceiling.

• As you exhale, sweep both hands around and down in a circular movement until they're at your side.

• Lengthen your spine, roll your shoulders back and relax.

Crystal Prescription

Sensual Taurus is governed by the planet Venus, and love is at the heart of everything you do. From self-love to snuggling up with someone special, the pink planet casts its glow far and wide and gives you an artistic flair. Always determined, and sometimes set in your ways, you need crystals that will help you find flexibility and ways to express your emotions.

Citrine

Known as the cuddle quartz, citrine is the perfect pick-me-up to boost confidence and help you feel secure. Also associated with prosperity, this vibrant stone taps into the Taurean need for abundance, so it's a win-win choice!

Hold the crystal in both hands and imagine being cloaked in the golden energy of the stone.

Turquoise

Taurus governs the throat and this colourful stone is associated with the throat chakra, so it helps you to express yourself and ignite your creative spark.

Wear as a pendant throughout your day.

Daily Stress Busters

Monday
Lose yourself in a book; it's a great way to get away from it all and take a well-earned break.

Tuesday
Put on your favourite dance track and boogie around the living room, shaking away any tension.

Wednesday
Take a blank sheet of paper and a pencil and free your imagination. From poetry to drawing or doodling, just enjoy being creative in some way.

Thursday
As an Earth sign, a trip to the countryside or a walk in the park is an instant mood booster. Be mindful as you explore; engage all your senses and connect with the landscape.

Friday
Sniff a lemon or burn a citrus-scented candle. The fresh, zesty fragrance ignites your sensual Taurean nature and brings clarity.

Saturday
Nurture your creative side and your love of food by baking a cake. Don't rush it – enjoy!

Sunday
Give yourself a mini facial with your favourite moisturizer and take time and care massaging it into your skin.

Taurus Self-love Ritual

It's time to abandon self-doubt and see yourself as others do.

• Stand in front of the mirror and look yourself in the eye.

• Hold your gaze and admire the loveliness of your face.

• Smile and notice how it lights up your features.

• Recognize that you are utterly unique and beautiful, as you are.

• Say, 'I love myself, just as I am.'

• Say it with feeling and confidence and keep repeating it until you really mean it.

Daily Empowering Meditation

Picture yourself standing before a cluster of trees. They reach up to the sky with gnarled branches that meet in a canopy above your head. The sun glistens through the boughs, sending tendrils of light to dance about the forest floor. You walk forwards and press your hands against the bark of the nearest trunk. The wood feels rough, the ridges digging into your palms. You breathe in and sense the tree's energy. You breathe out and feel the soles of your feet pressing into the Earth. You turn, rest your back against the trunk and feel a gentle tug along your spine. It's as if you're growing, reaching upwards, like a sapling searching for air and sunlight. Breathe in and feel energized, breathe out and feel strong.

Soothing Thyme for Taurus

Thyme is a multi-purpose herb that's easy to grow in a tub or garden. The scent is uplifting, and it's often used in tinctures to promote positive thinking. Packed full of vitamin C, it improves the immune system and promotes digestion.

To make a soothing cup of thyme tea, simmer a handful of fresh thyme sprigs in a pan of boiling water for about ten minutes. Strain the mixture into a cup, stir in a spoonful of honey, then enjoy.

Mindful Moment of Pampering

A long soak in the bath is the perfect way to revive your spirits.

Run yourself a bath and add a couple of drops of geranium essential oil, which helps to balance emotions. Relax and immerse yourself in the bubbles. Close your eyes and take a moment to inhale the gentle aroma and let it infuse you with positive energy. Feel the water as it laps against your skin. Notice how the warmth makes each muscle relax. Bring your attention to your breathing, to the softness of your chest. Let any thoughts or feelings flow through your mind. Just be in the moment and enjoy the experience.

A Good Night's Sleep

The stress you hang on to can resurface at night and disrupt your sleep. Even if you nod off, you might wake up fretting in the early hours. Let go of any worries and disengage from your day with a breathing exercise before bed.

• In a seated position, close your eyes and place your hands with palms facing upwards on your lap.

• Take a deep breath in and imagine you're drawing in peace through each hand. Feel this soothing energy fill your lungs, travel up your spine and into your head.

• As you exhale, imagine all the worry and stress of the day filtering from your body, as it pours from the centre of each hand and diffuses out into the air.

• With every breath you feel lighter and more relaxed as you continue to inhale peace and exhale stress.

Gemini

21 May–20 June

Element
Air

Planet
Mercury

Gemini Stars
Tom Holland (1 June)
Marilyn Monroe (1 June)
Venus Williams (17 June)

Mantra
'Positivity flows where
my heart goes.'

The Essence of Gemini

Versatile, vivacious and super-spontaneous, you're hard to pin down, Gemini, and that's just how you like it. There's nothing you enjoy more than surprising people with your knowledge and flair. Being the sign of the twins makes you full of contradictions. From erratic mood swings to simply going off-grid every now and then, you need your me-time, and you can find it hard to keep things on an even keel. Curiosity is where it's at: you love to learn new things, if only so that you can teach them to others. People interest you and you will throw yourself into group activities, but while you like the buzz of an active social life, there's a part of you that craves serenity. When you recognize your needs and go with the flow, you truly soar above the clouds.

Your Self-care Plan

You need to balance the different sides of your psyche. Your fun-loving, always-on-the-go persona is often at cross purposes with your quieter half, but here you will find rituals to appeal to your changeable nature and help them work in harmony. A quick fix to fire the imagination or a technique to calm body and mind, breathing tips to lull you into sleep, and suggestions to boost vitality – they are all here.

Morning Ritual to Get Up and Glow

• Stand in the shower and close your eyes.

• Turn up the power for a few seconds, let the water hit the top of your head. As it does, visualize a shower of energy surging through your body.

• Allow it to flush out fear, worry and confusion.

• Feel the water refresh you, ready for the day ahead.

Crystal Prescription

Being gregarious comes naturally to you, but there are times when it's hard work. People expect you to be entertaining and chatty, and while you're happy to oblige, you do suffer with bouts of low energy. Your perfect stones work to your strengths and bring equilibrium and vitality when they are most needed. Typical to your sign, you'll need different crystals at different times, and you should follow your heart when choosing them.

Kyanite

This beautiful, blue-tinted stone will help balance both sides of your personality. It has a grounding and motivating energy, so it will keep you on track with career goals.

Hold with both hands clasped together to align both sides of your psyche and induce calm.

Moonstone

A stone which channels the energy of the moon, this luminous crystal balances the emotions and keeps mood swings at bay. Make it your first choice when you need to maintain a positive mindset.

Place beneath your pillow for a rejuvenating night's sleep.

Daily Stress Busters

Monday
Hug a tree, or simply lean your back against the trunk and feel it supporting you.

Tuesday
Think of a time when you were happy and at peace. Walk through the memory in your mind, engaging all your senses and re-living the emotions.

Wednesday
Write a list of things you need to do and tick them off one by one. This will keep your mind on track and stop the Gemini need to procrastinate.

Thursday
Massage the spot in the centre of your forehead using circular movements to relieve tension and restore clarity.

Friday
Embrace your air element and go for a walk on a windy day. Stand in an exposed spot, close your eyes and feel each gust of wind cleansing and refreshing you.

Saturday
Look at the Yin-Yang symbol and see how the opposites are in perfect balance, then think about your own characteristics and how they make you the perfect whole.

Sunday
Visit somewhere you've never been before and take photos to create a picture storyboard of the event.

Gemini Self-love Ritual

You might be sociable, but you also enjoy moments of tranquillity. Delight your senses and have some me-time with this calming ritual.

• Light a scented candle - sandalwood, patchouli or black pepper are all lovely grounding fragrances.

• Spend a few minutes gazing at the flame to calm your mind.

• Close your eyes and inhale the sweet, earthy aroma. Let it wash over you like a blanket of calm.

• Picture a tiny flame beneath your belly button. This spark represents your self-esteem.

• Imagine it swelling until it fills your body with warmth and love.

Daily Enabling Meditation

You are sitting upon golden sand. In the distance you can hear the soft melody of children's laughter. The sea is calm, a sparkling azure blanket. The waves gently ebb and flow. You relax, feel your stomach and chest soften. A trickle of wind ruffles your hair, but you are warm and safe in this sanctuary, a place where you can simply be. The sounds in your head have gone. All is quiet. It is only you and the glorious sun, bathing you in a luminous glow. With every breath you feel strong, centred and buzzing with energy.

Restorative Fennel for Gemini

With its liquorice taste, fennel is a powerful herb with a host of medicinal properties. The ancient Greeks and Romans ate it for strength, but today it's thought to boost metabolism and detoxify the body. It's the go-to herb for Gemini, as it helps eliminate stress.

To make a restorative fennel infusion, slice a small piece of fresh ginger root, add to a pan of boiling water and simmer for five minutes. Crush a tablespoon of fennel seeds in a pestle and mortar. Remove the pan from the heat, add the fennel and leave for five minutes, then strain the liquid into a cup. Stir in a spoonful of honey, close your eyes and savour the taste.

Mindful Moment to Declutter

Your active mind can often be filled with conflicting thoughts. Clear the clutter and find peace by tapping into the element of air.

Every day, find a moment to stop and focus on your breathing. Draw the air deep into your lungs and imagine it filling your body with light and energy. As you inhale, picture your breath like a gust of wind, bursting through your body and clearing away negative energy. It sweeps through your head and pushes away doubt and fear. As you exhale, picture it like a vacuum of air being sucked from your body, taking with it all the debris that you no longer need.

A Good Night's Sleep

Geminis often suffer with insomnia and have erratic sleep patterns. Some nights you'll get plenty of sleep and others, hardly any. Regulate your sleep by introducing a bedtime meditation into your night-time routine.

• Find a comfortable spot to sit, close your eyes and focus on your breathing.

• Imagine yourself breathing in calmness and releasing anxiety.

• As you inhale, repeat the word 'calm' in your mind.

• See it as a colour, perhaps white or silver, and imagine you are bathed in this hue.

• Notice any tension in your body. If a muscle feels tight, imagine breathing your chosen colour into it.

• Do this with every part of your body until you feel totally relaxed.

Cancer

21 June–22 July

Element
Water

Planet
Moon

Cancer Stars
Lana Del Rey (21 June)
Princess Diana (1 July)
Frida Kahlo (6 July)

Mantra
'I am perfect as I am.'

The Essence of Cancer

Intuitive and deeply mystical, you take it all to heart, Cancer. A sensitive soul, you easily pick up on atmospheres and know when someone is hurting. Being a natural care-giver, you'll stop at nothing to protect your nearest and dearest, even if that means putting yourself in harm's way. Home is your sanctuary, a place to recharge and reboot from the day's stresses, and you love nothing more than making it a cosy refuge. Those who don't know you might think you're distant, but the air of indifference is just a way to protect yourself from getting hurt. In truth, you're one of the biggest softies of the zodiac. Your hard shell is a cover and when you crack, you're a torrent of emotion. It's no wonder that opening up can be difficult, but on the flip side, it's good to get things off your chest before it affects your mood and your health. When you feel safe and able to express yourself creatively, you're the most captivating crab on the beach.

Your Self-care Plan

Your plan needs to allow you to be sensitive and caring, but strengthen your inner core and keep you centred. You naturally absorb the feelings of others, so you need to be able to release any negative energy in a way that works for you. These rituals will fit in with your daily routine and make you more positive. From uplifting meditations to simple tips that promote stability, you'll feel calm, energized and ready to heal the world.

Morning Ritual to Get Up and Glow

• Stand with feet hip-width apart, shoulders relaxed, and place your hands on your hips.

• Bend forwards from the waist as far as is comfortable, then return to a standing position.

• Bend backwards from the waist, until you feel a gentle pull, then return to standing.

• Twist from the waist, side to side, for a minute. Pick up speed a little and see how far you can turn, but don't strain yourself.

• Say, 'I am flexible, adaptable and I go with the flow.'

Crystal Prescription

You're a side-stepper when it comes to avoiding confrontation, just like your crab counterpart, but it means you often keep the bad stuff inside. While airing your grievances might be difficult, harbouring them is hard on you. Crystals can help you feel strong, centred and able to express yourself, while you boost your intuitive nature.

Labradorite

This rainbow-coloured stone is linked to intuition. It will hone your sixth sense and promote clear communication between yourself and others. It also dispels negativity.

Hold over the middle of your forehead, breathe deeply and let your thoughts flow.

Smoky Quartz

This stone oozes strength and stability. It banishes negative vibes and works to boost confidence and self-belief.

Wear daily as a pendant close to the skin to feel empowered.

Daily Stress Busters

Monday
Cancerians are deep thinkers, so set yourself a challenge to learn a new language or skill.

Tuesday
Visualize a protective shell around you. See it as a golden shield, which allows loving energy in, but rebounds anything negative.

Wednesday
Add a couple of drops of rosemary essential oil to your bath. This refreshing scent is empowering and will dispel worry.

Thursday
Have a laugh. Watch a funny movie or have a giggle with friends.

Friday
As a water sign, you're naturally drawn to the ocean, but if you can't get to the coast, a walk along the riverbank will also invigorate you.

Saturday
Connect with your planet. Stand beneath the light of the Moon, close your eyes and bask in its illuminating glow.

Sunday
Strengthen your core and your spirit. Lay on the floor with your legs bent. Pull your tummy in and hold for a few seconds. Release and repeat five times.

Cancer Self-love Ritual

You can be hard on yourself and tend to dwell on the negative, but it's time to celebrate the amazing person that you are.

• Take a sheet of paper and make a list of ten qualities or things that you love about yourself – anything from the way you smile to your compassionate nature. If you find this hard, ask a friend or family member to help.

• Read through the list and acknowledge that you are fantastic.

• Keep the paper with you and read it when you need a reminder, as a self-care exercise.

Daily Uplifting Meditation

You are standing on a riverbank; the water is flowing at your feet.
You gaze into the inky blue depths and feel a sense of wonder.
The ripples create spirals on the surface as the water moves, and
the beautiful patterns focus your mind. You step forward; suddenly,
the urge to submerge yourself takes over. You dive in, feel the cool
liquid against your skin. You take a deep gulp of air as your head
emerges. The river welcomes you in a gentle embrace and every pore
tingles with excitement. A wave of energy pulsates through your
body and you begin to swim. Heading into the flow, you move with
ease. Refreshed and centred, you are ready to take on the world.
Breathe, smile and relax...

Cleansing Sage for Cancer

Packed full of medicinal properties, sage is a great all-rounder, full of antioxidants and associated with cleansing. It's also thought to improve brain function and memory. Linked to the Moon, it's the perfect cure-all and will help to clear negative thinking patterns.

To make a cleansing sage smudge stick, cut about ten sprigs of fresh sage and four sprigs of lavender to the same length and bundle them together. Fix securely at the base by tying with twine, then continue to wrap this around the full length of the stick, pulling the sprigs tightly together. Tie and hang the stick for at least two weeks to dry. To use, light the end of the stick so it gently smoulders and carefully waft the scented smoke around your body, inhale, relax and invite the positive energy in.

Mindful Moment of Emotion

Choose a moment and stop what you are doing. Stand or sit in silence and assess how you feel.

Start by turning your attention to the centre of your chest. Feel your heart beating, and the gentle rise and fall of your diaphragm as you breathe. Notice how your body continues to do what it needs to do without you thinking about it. Breathe in deeply and ask yourself how you feel right now. Are you calm, stressed, emotional, centred? Give this feeling a word in your mind. Exhale. Now ask how you want to feel, and as you inhale, breathe in the sentiment of that word.

A Good Night's Sleep

Worrying is something of an art form to you, and at night when all is quiet, your fretting turns up a gear. Switch the focus of your thoughts with a super-relaxing night-time ritual that will lighten your cares.

• Slow your breathing down by counting out each breath and taking your time.

• Turn your attention to the area behind your eyes. Imagine it's a room full of boxes. Each box contains a worry or a fear.

• Take it in turns to zap each box in your mind so that it disappears, until you're left with a large, white, open space.

• Breathe in the emptiness.

• Relax and know that you can return to this peaceful state at any point during the night.

Leo

23 July–22 August

Element
Fire

Planet
Sun

Leo Stars
Louis Armstrong (4 August)
Mata Hari (7 August)
Madonna (16 August)

Mantra
'It is okay to simply be.'

The Essence of Leo

There's no mistaking a Leo; you are bold, vibrant and full of energy. You command attention, and that's okay because people flock to you, but while leadership comes naturally, you're also a pussy cat at heart. When you love, you're all in; there are no half measures. Cheerful and proactive, you'll go the extra mile if it helps in your quest for world domination. How you look is important – it's all about image – but that also means you get caught up in what others think. Beneath the devil-may-care attitude is a heart of gold and a sensitive soul. You're not short on confidence and you always try to see the positives, but all this charm takes effort, which occasionally leaves you running on empty. Give yourself a break and let the façade slip. Being popular is fun, but being kind to yourself will also make you feel like number one.

Your Self-care Plan

Your plan is all about acknowledging your softer side. Beneath the vibrant and outgoing exterior, you long to be understood. The techniques here work to your strengths and infuse you with power, but also allow you to reveal your softer nature. You'll find tips for self-kindness and letting the love flow, and rituals to help you shine by tapping into the energy of your governing planet, the Sun.

Morning Ritual to Get Up and Glow

Get your mystic mojo on with this ritual to hone your intuitive skills.

• Close your eyes and breathe deeply. Focus your attention on the centre of your forehead; imagine there's a beautiful purple flowerbud sitting in this spot.

• Take a long breath in and as you exhale, picture the bud slowly beginning to unfurl.

• With every breath, the petals curl outwards until the flower is fully open.

• This is the flower of your intuition. It will help you trust your instincts as you navigate the day ahead.

Crystal Prescription

There's no mistaking your sunny personality. Most people see the bravado and never know what tenderness lies behind. Yes, you need to be loved, but you also need to love and make genuine connections. Crystals that help you recharge and bring out your softer side are the way forward.

Rose Quartz

Known as the heart stone, this beautiful crystal is associated with loving energy. It opens the heart and helps to balance the emotions. Gently uplifting, it will calm your fiery moods and allow you to connect with others on a deeper level.

Close your eyes while holding this stone, and picture yourself bathed in a rosy pink glow.

Amber

Associated with life-giving energy, this stone is thought to promote vitality and recharge the batteries. It's also known to stimulate the immune system.

During downtime, sit with it, breathe and focus on its vibrant colour.

Daily Stress Busters

Monday
Cool your fiery ardour and de-stress by holding your wrists under cold running water for a couple of minutes.

Tuesday
Don't just tell a joke, perform it as if you're in front of an audience. Practise and refine it, then share it with friends and family.

Wednesday
Get into yoga. With the emphasis on breathing and balance, this is the perfect way for Leos to find peace.

Thursday
Imagine you're bathed in the Sun's life-giving rays. Feel the warmth hit the top of your head and shower you in energizing light.

Friday
Take a step back and slow things down. Pause, count to ten slowly and focus on the numbers. Switching your focus in this way will help you feel calm.

Saturday
Open up with some journalling. Write a paragraph and describe how you are feeling right now.

Sunday
Find a comfortable spot and watch the Sun rise. Enjoy this moment of tranquillity before the day begins.

Leo Self-love Ritual

You're so generous with others; use this ritual to remind you to be kind to yourself, too.

• Buy some flowers and arrange them in a vase.

• Sit and gaze at their beauty.

• Imagine you've bought them for a friend or relative. What would you write in the gift card? How would you let this person know how special they are to you?

• Say it to yourself, either out loud or in your head.

• Every time you look at the flowers, be reminded that you are a loving human being and perfect as you are.

Daily Strengthening Meditation

Imagine you are seated in the middle of a wildflower meadow. The Sun is high in the sky and the Earth is bathed in its glorious glow. Your hands are pressed firmly into the soft grass and you are surrounded by a riot of colour. Delicate flowers on tall stems reach up for their moment of glory. A ring of brilliant white and buttery yellow daisies surround you in a circle, like a spotlight. You smile, close your eyes and turn your face upwards so that you can feel the warmth of the rays on your skin. Nothing matters in this moment. You feel completely at peace, calm and ready for whatever comes your way. The Sun has you in its sights and you are golden.

Cooling Chamomile for Leo

Chamomile is a healing powerhouse. Associated with stress relief, it calms the body and mind, boosts the immune system and tackles insomnia. A natural sedative, it's the perfect Leo herb, as it thrives in the Sun and promotes inner peace.

To make a cooling chamomile iced tea, put a teaspoon of dried chamomile flowers in an infuser, place in a cup and steep in boiling water for around ten minutes. Remove the infuser and let the liquid cool. Add a squeeze of lemon and three or four ice cubes, then sip and unwind.

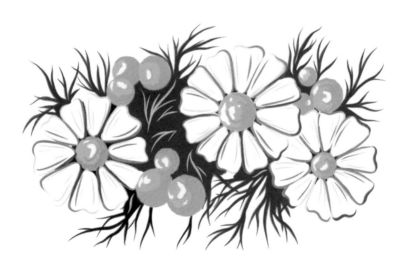

Mindful Moment to Observe

Being so dynamic, you move through life at a pace, but often miss what is under your nose.

Choose a moment to really look around you. Pick out one thing that you can see and focus on it. Next, think about what you can hear. Zone in and listen beyond the surface. Pick out one sound that you've not noticed before and let it play in your mind. Now think about what you can smell. Is the air fresh or littered with fragrance? Think of a word to describe the aroma. Turn your attention to what you can taste as you breathe. Do you notice anything unusual? Finally ask yourself, 'what can I feel?' Perhaps you feel the breeze against your skin, the earth beneath your feet? Pick out one thing and focus on it.

A Good Night's Sleep

Switching off is not normally a problem, but you can obsess over details, particularly when it comes to how others see you, which causes physical tension. This night-time ritual helps your body relax and will soothe you into sleep.

• Activate self-soothing with a moisturizing hand massage.

• Start with your hands, taking it in turn to rub in a little body lotion. Work in circular movements from the centre of the palm outwards and along each finger and thumb.

• Gently rotate the joints and stretch your fingers.

• Pay attention to how this feels and notice any stiffness or tingling.

• Continue up the arm on each side if you wish. You can also do the same to your feet, ankles and legs.

Virgo

23 August–22 September

Element
Earth

Planet
Mercury

Virgo Stars
Blake Lively (25 August)
Zendaya (1 September)
Michael Bublé (9 September)

Mantra
'I find joy right now
in this moment.'

The Essence of Virgo

Diligent and dedicated, you're the real deal, Virgo. You put the effort in, and combine logic and wit to get things done. Friends and family are important to you, and you'll do anything to raise a smile from your nearest and dearest. You're a perfectionist at heart, and while this means whatever you do, you do extra well, it also piles the pressure on. You can be self-critical and picky, and you tend to overthink things, which can leave you in a bit of whirl. Being a practical Earth sign, you're always on hand to help and can't bear to see others struggling. Your kind heart means you'll get involved when others would walk away. You like to be needed, but that often means you'll put your needs last. A co-operative atmosphere is the ideal scenario for you, and you thrive best when facing a challenge – that's when your inner superhero takes control!

Your Self-care Plan

Your plan is all about relaxation and rejuvenation. It takes time and effort to help others, especially to your high standards, leaving you scarcely a moment to breathe. These techniques will help you take a step back to quieten your mind and help you recognize your self-worth. Designed to fit in with your busy lifestyle, these techniques should work with your specific strengths and help you see how amazing and accomplished you are.

Morning Ritual to Get Up and Glow

Set your intention for the day with this morning ritual to put a spring in your step.

• Take a minute to sit, feet flat on the floor, shoulders relaxed.

• Ask yourself, 'what do I want to achieve today?'

• Visualize this happening in your mind, and breathe into the intention by taking a deep breath in.

• As you exhale, let the picture in your mind get bigger and brighter.

• Now ask yourself, 'how do I want to feel today?'

• Breathe into this intention and imagine that's how you feel right now.

Crystal Prescription

You are methodical in your approach to life and a problem solver. Your can-do attitude is admired by many, but it means that people come to rely on you. While you love to help, the extra pressure you put on yourself can take its toll. Crystals that encourage you to remain calm and centred are the way to go, along with stones that boost self-esteem and remind you that you are fabulous.

Sodalite

Often called the 'stone of peace', sodalite has a deeply calming effect on the mind. It keeps negative thoughts at bay, and will help you find stillness and strength when the world gets chaotic.

Pop a piece beneath your pillow at night, for a restful slumber.

Red Jasper

Although it has a fiery energy, this crystal motivates at a gentle pace. It's the stone of self-acceptance and will help critical Virgoans love themselves that little bit more.

Hold it in your dominant hand, breathe and draw in the stone's caring energy.

Daily Stress Busters

Monday
If your mind is in a frenzy, switch up your thinking. Shout 'Stop!' in your head, then focus on something that makes you smile, like your family or a favourite pastime.

Tuesday
Take a brisk walk. It doesn't matter where you are going, just get the lungs pumping, the air circulating and pick up your pace.

Wednesday
Do some gardening. Cultivate a patch or pot, plant some seeds and dig your hands deep in the soil. This is the perfect pick-me-up for Earth signs who enjoy connecting with the environment.

Thursday
Take a cat nap. You're a hardworking soul but even you need a break. Allow yourself five minutes to sit, close your eyes and do absolutely nothing.

Friday
Give yourself a pep talk. Bring to mind three things that you've achieved in the last few weeks. Small things count, even everyday tasks that you do without thinking. Then repeat 'I am awesome!' out loud or in your head three times.

Saturday
Set yourself a practical challenge, like putting up a shelf. Take your time and enjoy the process of making something.

Sunday
Stop what you are doing, sit back and listen to an uplifting song.

Virgo Self-love Ritual

You can become obsessed with helping others, but it's time to do something special for you.

• Run yourself a bath using bergamot or ylang ylang essential oils; both fragrances are known for their uplifting properties.

• Scatter rose petals on the surface to make it look special, then light some candles.

• Take your time, relax and soak in the soothing water. Don't rush the experience; this is about being kind to yourself.

• Close your eyes and immerse yourself below the surface for a few seconds. As you emerge, feel the stress slip from your body.

Daily Joyful Meditation

Imagine you are sitting in front of a roaring fire. The flames leap and twist and you are mesmerized. The colours glow with brightness: burnt orange and gold, and a hint of blue. Feel the heat against your skin. You gaze into the fire and a deep relaxation falls upon you like a comforting blanket. Waves of joy flood through your body. You take a deep breath in, and as you exhale you release all the worry that you have been carrying. The pressure to be perfect is gone in this one long breath. You smile and feel the spark of creativity burning within.

Creative Honeysuckle for Virgo

The flowers of the honeysuckle are an instant pick-me-up. With a sweet, calming aroma, it's a winner with your star sign. It has the power to trigger your intuition, helping you go with the flow and think creatively.

To make a honeysuckle spray to boost creativity, place a muslin (cheesecloth) in a bowl with the edges hanging over the side. Fill this with honeysuckle flowers and then cover with boiling water. Leave overnight to infuse. Gather up the four corners of the cloth and squeeze any water into the bowl. Pour into a pan and simmer for five minutes to reduce the liquid, then cool and decant into a spray bottle. Spritz on pulse points, clothes and soft furnishings to light your creative spark.

Mindful Moment to Connect

Feel those loving connections with your nearest and dearest.

Stop what you are doing and think of someone you care about. Look at a photo if it helps. Notice everything about them, from their appearance to their expression. Look at the warmth in their eyes and how their personality shines through in everything they do. As you breathe in, imagine sending this person all your love. Picture the two of you wrapped up in a hug. Relax and give thanks for their reassuring presence in your life.

A Good Night's Sleep

You adore your shut-eye, Virgo, but when the lights go out you can find it hard to switch off. Instead of relaxing, you pick apart the events of the day. Turn the tables and embrace the positive with this calming night-time ritual.

• As you lay in bed, take a deep breath in, hold for the count of four, then release.

• Say out loud, or in your head, 'Today was a good day because ...' then fill in the gap. Think of something that happened that made you smile and focus on how you felt at the time.

• Take another deep breath in, hold for the count of four, and then release.

• Say, 'I drift to sleep happy that my day is complete.'

Libra

23 September–22 October

Element
Air

Planet
Venus

Libra Stars
Gwyneth Paltrow (27 September)
Zac Efron (18 October)
Kim Kardashian (21 October)

Mantra
'I have a clear vision
of where I need to be.'

The Essence of Libra

Appropriately for the sign of the scales, your life is a balancing act, Libra, and you do it with grace. With your bright smile, you're a beacon of positive energy – it's no wonder people flock to you. While you try to share the love, you do have down days and, being the natural peacemaker of the zodiac, you're always trying to keep everyone happy. Juggling plates is your speciality, but it puts pressure on you, which can take its toll. You may be a superhero and able to solve most problems, but sometimes you have to disconnect and take a step back. Luckily, you've got a great sense of humour and appreciate the finer things in life, thanks to your ruler Venus. When you're on top form, you're a class act – poised, centred and ready to sparkle.

Your Self-care Plan

Your plan complements your Libran ability to see both sides, but also helps you follow your heart and take action. Techniques that improve focus and boost self-confidence will help you flourish. Libran rituals are designed to fit in with your love of beauty, while helping you take a moment to find inner stillness. True insight is born in these moments of quiet. From boosting energy levels to eliminating worry before bedtime, this is the perfect strategy to unleash your star quality.

Morning Ritual to Get Up and Glow

• Close your eyes and breathe deeply.

• Imagine you are sitting before a giant cinema screen showing a movie of your day ahead.

• See yourself going about your business with a smile.

- Picture yourself at the end of the day, happy and relaxed. You have achieved everything and all is well.

- Remember that however the day pans out, you've got this.

Crystal Prescription

As a level-headed lovely you like to consider all your options, which works well when working in a team environment but can prove difficult when you have key decisions to make. Librans sometimes get bogged down in detail and clarity evades them. You're a natural people-pleaser but can lose your own sense of direction. Crystals that cleanse the mind and spirit and help you to focus are ideal.

Hematite

This stone has the power to bring you back down to earth and also clear the mind of clutter. It amplifies positive energy and will help you make clear decisions and put them into action.

Carry one in your pocket when you're feeling stressed.

Blue Lace Agate

With Venus as your governing planet, you can sometimes get obsessed with how things appear on the surface. This spiritual stone has a calming energy that will help you look for deeper meaning and see the beauty around you.

Close your eyes and meditate while holding the stone, or pop it under your pillow for inspiring dreams.

Daily Stress Busters

Monday
Clear your mind by taking five minutes to focus on your breathing. Every time a thought pops up, return your attention to the rise and fall of your chest.

Tuesday
Write a list of five things that you are grateful for.

Wednesday
Treat yourself to your favourite beauty treatment, whether it's a luxurious facial or a pampering pedicure.

Thursday
Improve your posture. Stand tall, with your shoulders back, your feet hip-width apart and your chin slightly tilted. Lengthen your tailbone and extend your spine upwards.

Friday
Videocall a friend to re-connect and activate feel-good vibes.

Saturday
Stand in front of a mirror and say, 'I am beautiful and brilliant, because ....' then let the compliments flow.

Sunday
Visit your favourite coffee shop and choose something different from the menu.

Libra Self-love Ritual

You always see the good in others, but now it's time for you. Recognize your self-worth with this esteem-boosting ritual.

• Write yourself a love letter.

• It doesn't have to be long but take the time and care to say what you really feel.

• Imagine you are talking to your younger self and address yourself with kindness.

• Look at where you are now and all the wonderful things that you have achieved.

• Celebrate the brilliant person you've become and all the amazing things you are yet to do.

Daily Vibrant Meditation

Imagine you are sitting at the top of a mountain. It is early morning and the Sun is peeping over the horizon. The hills and valleys ripple beneath those first rays of light. It's a gradual process as the Sun climbs higher in the sky and you track its movement. You take a deep breath in and feel the warmth hit the top of your head; it falls like a shower and bathes you in golden brightness. The heat permeates your skin. It infuses you with power and you feel energized and ready to face the day. You stretch your arms upwards and bring your hands together above your head. Your entire body is buzzing with vitality. You breathe in the Sun's light and, as you exhale, you feel any worries slip from your shoulders.

Energizing Eucalyptus for Libra

Fresh and vibrant, eucalyptus cut throughs the atmosphere, lifting the vibes and clearing the air. The fragrance has the power to clear stagnant energy and boost the mood. Associated with the planet Venus, it's the perfect Libran pick-me-up.

To make an energizing eucalyptus room spray, fill a small spray bottle with distilled water and about eight drops of eucalyptus essential oil. Seal the lid and give a gentle shake to mix the ingredients. Spritz around your home to promote positive energy.

Mindful Moment for the Senses

Stop and see the wonder in the world right in front of you.

Whether you're at work or home, start the process by saying 'stop' in your mind and silencing internal chatter, then engage your senses and take in what you can see, hear, smell, taste, touch and feel. Really look at the shapes and colours that dance before your eyes. Become a tourist in your own life and imagine you are seeing these things for the first time. How do you feel? What word springs to mind to describe the experience. Breathe, relax and enjoy the beauty of your daily life.

A Good Night's Sleep

You like to keep body and mind in balance, but at night thoughts can drift into your head and prevent you from getting your sleep. A simple ritual to release niggling worries will help you find the peace you need.

• Keep a pad and pen by your bed. Before you turn in for the evening, write down anything that is bothering you. Try to stick to simple sentences, or words that sum up your thoughts.

• When you've finished, screw or tear the paper up and throw it in a wastepaper bin.

• Say, 'I release all thoughts and concerns. My mind is clear of worry.'

• If you wake in the night and find your mind is whirling, repeat the process to get rid of unnecessary thoughts.

Scorpio

23 October–21 November

Element
Water

Planet
Mars

Scorpio Stars
Emma Stone (6 November)
Marie Curie (7 November)
Whoopi Goldberg (13 November)

Mantra
'My roots are grounded,
but I bend in the breeze.'

The Essence of Scorpio

Enigmatic and individual, you've got it all going on, Scorpio, including that famous sting in the tail. Cool composure is where it's at with you, at least on the surface. Like a swan gliding on water you appear serene, but beneath it all is a passionate powerhouse of potential. A natural leader, your forthright attitude means that everyone knows exactly where they stand. That said, you can be trusted with secrets, and if someone seeks you out, you're a caring confidante. Your bravery and determination give you the edge, and once you've made up your mind about something or someone, it takes a lot to change it. Despite being a water sign, you're fixed in your ways, and find it hard to trust others. Yes, you're one tough cookie, but that's how you like it. It can be difficult to forge deep relationships when you're in cautious mode, and your habit of keeping things to yourself doesn't help. When you do open up to others, you're like an exotic flower, intoxicating and truly unforgettable.

Your Self-care Plan

Your plan needs to complement your enigmatic leadership skills, and help you move forward with flexibility. These rituals encourage you to go with the flow and take your time before making decisions. Your charismatic personality acts like a magnet, but to really make the most of your potential you need to find balance and relinquish some control. Your plan will help you switch from work to relaxation mode, and engage in a mindful way with the world around you.

Morning Ritual to Get Up and Glow

• Sit on the floor, with your back leaning against the wall.

• Place both hands over your heart and take a deep breath in through your nose.

• Exhale through the mouth, and as you do so, imagine your heart radiating loving energy to the rest of your body.

• Continue to breathe in this way with the focus on the centre of your chest.

• Picture this uplifting energy as a pink light that fills you with vitality.

Crystal Prescription

Dynamic and decisive, you're unstoppable when you've set your heart on something. While these qualities help you get ahead, they can hinder progress on a personal level. When your mind is made up, you rarely budge, and you find it hard to be objective. Choose crystals that promote positivity and help you look beyond the surface and see both sides.

Lapis Lazuli

This gorgeous stone promotes awareness and understanding by bringing mental clarity, and has an invigorating energy that will lift your spirits.

Hold over your throat for a few minutes every day to help you communicate from the heart.

Kunzite

This stone is thought to heal and balance the emotions. It's also associated with unconditional love and will help you empathize with others.

Carry one in your pocket to help you find moments of peace during your day.

Daily Stress Busters

Monday
Set yourself a practical baking challenge to follow a recipe. It will appeal to the Scorpio's competitive streak and help you chill out.

Tuesday
Run on the spot for three minutes. Start with a gentle jog, then build up to a minute of fast running, lifting your knees up to your chest, then cool down with a slow walk.

Wednesday
Give yourself an invigorating head massage. Hang your head upside down and knead your scalp for a couple of minutes.

Thursday
Imagine you're an alien visiting Earth. Look at your surroundings as though you are seeing them for the first time. What do you notice?

Friday
Close your eyes and sip a chilled glass of water. Focus on how this feels and tastes.

Saturday
Take an energizing shower. Close your eyes and notice how the water feels against your skin then, for the last few seconds, turn the temperature down.

Sunday
Create a moodboard of what you'd like to achieve over the next week. Have fun using pictures, drawings and quotes.

Scorpio Self-love Ritual

As strange as it sounds, self-soothing by touch can help alleviate stress and give you the loving boost you deserve.

• Sit on the floor with your knees bent.

• Find a soft snuggly blanket and drape it over your shoulders.

• Wrap your arms around your knees and close your eyes.

• If you prefer, cross your arms over your chest and hold the opposite shoulder.

• As you cuddle yourself, say, 'I am loved.'

• Relax, and slow your breathing.

Daily Flexibility Meditation

Imagine you are standing in a wood. You are surrounded by trees and gaze up into the leafy canopy and the patterns of the branches. Your naked feet press into the damp earth and you feel a connection with the landscape. It's as if you are rooted, anchored to the spot. The wind blows, rustling through the leaves; you can feel it against your skin. Your body sways with the breeze but still you stand firm; the soles of your feet have sunk deep into the soil. It doesn't matter how much you bend or stretch, the Earth holds you safe. You breathe in and draw strength. You breathe out and find flexibility.

Soothing Nettle for Scorpio

Nettles are packed with nutrients and are known to ease aching joints and promote blood flow. A plant powerhouse, they're the ideal pick-me-up for Scorpios. They grow in abundance, but if you want to avoid getting stung, you can gain as much benefit from pre-packaged herbal teas.

To make a soothing nettle bath soak, put a nettle tea bag in a bowl with a handful of dandelion flower heads, cover with boiling water and leave to steep for five minutes. Scoop out the tea bag and the flowers, then add the soak to running bath water. As you relax in the warm bath, close your eyes and inhale the earthy aroma.

Mindful Moment to Cleanse

Use your governing element, water, to clear the mind and bring you back to the moment.

Fill the sink with cold water, take a deep breath and dip your fingers in. Notice the temperature and how it makes your skin tingle. Watch as the water envelops each finger. Breathe deeply and immerse your hands to the wrist. Continue to take slow, deep breaths and enjoy the sensations. Wriggle and flex your fingers. Feel the pull of water against them. Take a final deep breath and imagine you are drawing in the cleansing energy of the water. Pull the plug, and watch as the sink clears, then give your hands a good shake.

A Good Night's Sleep

You're not prone to late-night worrying, but you are always thinking about your next move. It can be hard for you to switch from work mode to sleep mode, but a ritual that quietens the mind can help.

• Add three drops of lavender essential oil to an oil burner, or a small bowl of hot water, and place on your bedside table.

• Sit on the edge of the bed, close your eyes and inhale through the nose.

• Exhale through your mouth to the count of five.

• Inhale the gentle aroma.

• Exhale and feel each part of your body relax, starting with your head, neck and shoulders and then moving down to your feet.

Sagittarius

22 November–21 December

Element
Fire

Planet
Jupiter

Sagittarius Stars
Taylor Swift (13 December)
Jane Austen (16 December)
Jake Gyllenhaal (19 December)

Mantra
'Each day is an opportunity
for me to grow.'

The Essence of Sagittarius

As an athletically gifted Sagittarius, you're more than just a sporting hero; you shine with the exuberance of one who knows their worth. Your independent spirit takes you far, both physically and mentally. There are no limitations for you. Freedom is your favourite word and you make the most of it. With an up-for-anything attitude, you'll throw yourself into new projects and venture well beyond your comfort zone. Socially you flourish and have a wide group of friends. Being a butterfly, you're not heavy on commitment but you do benefit from one-to-one closeness as long as you're not stifled. You always go for what you want, but you can take things to heart and this affects your mood and energy levels. Your spontaneous nature makes it hard for you to slow down. Taking a moment to breathe and engage your senses will help with decision-making and develop your intuition too.

Your Self-care Plan

The best plan for you complements your spontaneous streak by infusing you with energy, but calming you down when you need to recharge. While you hate to slow down, you can't blaze a trail if you burn yourself out. Your plan is designed to help you establish the balance and work to your unique strengths. You'll find inspiring exercises to set you up for the day and boost motivation, along with tips to bring out your compassionate side.

Morning Ritual to Get Up and Glow

• Connect with the Earth's energy and think of yourself as a sapling buried deep in the ground.

• Curl into a tight ball. Tuck in your head and legs and place your hands flat to support you.

• Slowly push up with your hands and rise to your feet. Imagine you are a shoot bursting from the soil and unfurl to a standing position.

• Roll up onto your tiptoes. Stretch your arms upwards and feel the tug along your spine.

Crystal Prescription

Humour is your superpower and you use it to navigate the highs and lows of life, but you sometimes forget how your words affect others. Sagittarian skin is notoriously thick, but not everyone is built the same. Crystals that nurture your compassionate side and activate intuitive skills are ideal.

Rhodonite

A beautiful stone, with loving energy, rhodonite encourages you to reach out to others and empathize with them. It's also a stone of balance, inducing peace and tranquillity.

Rub it in the centre of your palm when you're feeling tense.

Carnelian

This joyful stone exudes positivity, promotes self-awareness and clarity. The uplifting energy won't stifle your spirit of adventure, but it will help you think things through and see the bigger picture.

Hold in both hands and meditate upon the vibrant colour of the stone.

Daily Stress Busters

Monday
Take a couple of minutes to gaze at the sky. Drink in the colours and notice how they blend. Look for any movement, from birds flying to the clouds changing shape.

Tuesday
Add rose-scented oil to an infuser, close your eyes and inhale the sweet aroma.

Wednesday
Get a pad and pen and doodle. Let your mind wander, and let the pen take over. Have fun and create patterns and shapes, then marvel at your artistry.

Thursday
You are naturally unpredictable, so flip the switch to turn on measured thinking with a logical puzzle, like sudoku or a crossword.

Friday
Light a candle and watch the flame for a few minutes to calm and focus your mind.

Saturday
Write a poem for someone you care about. It doesn't have to be perfect but make it heart-felt.

Sunday
Indulge your adventurous side and go for a mindful walk or run somewhere you've never been before.

Sagittarius Self-love Ritual

Cherish the good things in your life with a self-love practice that boosts positive energy.

• Start a self-love journal and fill it with things that make you feel good, from uplifting poems to counting your blessings.

• Include your favourite memories and write about the special people in your life.

• Add to the journal every week to reinforce positive vibes.

• Dip into it whenever you need a pick-me-up.

Daily Inspiring Meditation

Visualize yourself sitting on a hilltop at night. All is quiet and calm. A small fire flickers in front of you. At first the flames are just embers, specks of light in the darkness, but with every breath they grow bigger and brighter. Soon the fire is blazing and you are bathed in the amber glow. Your skin tingles from the heat, and your entire body is relaxed. You look up and see the stars twinkling in the sky above. The blanket of darkness protects you, and you feel centred and strong. From your vantage point, you can see in every direction and you know that you can go anywhere and be anything. The power to achieve your dreams is at your fingertips. Breathe in the light. Breathe out the darkness.

Refreshing Mint for Sagittarius

Mint is calming for your active body and mind. It helps to soothe an upset stomach and quieten mind-chatter, while its antibacterial properties cleanse and bring clarity. Easy to grow, this versatile herb can be kept in a pot on your window ledge.

To make a refreshing mint tea, put a handful of mint leaves in a pan of boiling water and infuse for five minutes. Strain into a cup, add some lemon slices or a dash of lemon juice, then sip and savour this restorative brew.

Mindful Moment of Creativity

Ignite your creative spark to help you think in new ways.

Stop and look out of the window. Pick one thing to focus on, then think of three sentences to describe it. Go for the first words that come into your mind and write them down. Take five long, deep breaths and look again at your chosen object. Now challenge yourself to describe it in a new way. Engage your imagination and focus on the true nature of the object. Think about its purpose and if it reminds you of anything. How does it make you feel? Write three more sentences. Compare what you have written and notice how each description brings the object to life in a different way.

A Good Night's Sleep

You're a restless sleeper and no wonder. Snoozing seems like a waste of time to a thrill-seeker like you so, to avoid burnout, think of a good night's rest as the fuel to fire your adventures.

• Lay down and close your eyes.

• Imagine you are standing at the top of a giant staircase. Inhale deeply, then exhale deeply as you slowly take each step down.

• With every step you take, you feel your body sink further into the bed.

• Let each muscle relax fully and continue to take the stairs until you reach a point where you feel calm and sleepy.

Capricorn

22 December–19 January

Element
Earth

Planet
Saturn

Capricorn Stars
Jared Leto (26 December)
Kit Harrington (26 December)
Nigella Lawson (6 January)

Mantra
'I breathe in peace,
I release stress.'

The Essence of Capricorn

Capable and canny, you're something of a genius, Capricorn. A practical soul, you can turn your hand to almost anything. Slow and steady wins the race, and where other signs might fall at the first hurdle, you'll plough doggedly on to the finish. You're not afraid to take responsibility, which makes you a good lead, and many people are in awe of your can-do approach. That said, you're often seen as serious, and can appear aloof. It's not that you don't care, quite the opposite, you care too much and when things go wrong you take it personally and find it hard to let go of the past. You can struggle with self-guilt but when you do relax, your funny side shines through and wins you an army of admirers. An environment where you feel appreciated is what pleases you most.

Your Self-care Plan

Your plan will encourage you to banish self-doubt and implement a pattern of positive thinking to help you lead with confidence. This, coupled with your capable, resourceful nature, will help you live your best life. These rituals are designed to boost self-belief and help you generate positive energy, complementing your latent gifts while slotting into your busy schedule. You'll find tips for self-kindness, exercises that promote flexibility and an empowering meditation to help you reach your full potential.

Morning Ritual to Get Up and Glow

• Stand with your feet hip-width apart, then stretch them wider.

• Place your hands on your hips and begin to twist. Start gently then twist further each time.

• Pick up speed and feel the stretch at your waist.

• Extend your arms outwards to give each twist more power.

• Repeat this affirmation, 'I am flexible and adaptable!'. Continue for a minute, then slow down to a gradual stop.

Crystal Prescription

Your practical nature means you rarely get side-tracked and problems don't usually faze you. It's easy to apply yourself to a task, and while you're fully engaged, you're happy. Should your mind wander you can fall into negative thinking patterns and doubt your abilities. Choose crystals that keep you calm and focused.

Howlite

Gentle and calming, howlite is the perfect antidote to an over-active mind. It also promotes sleep and aids patience.

Place over the centre of your forehead, breathe and relax.

Quartz

Known as the 'master healer', quartz has a vibrant energy that dispels toxins and balances the emotions. It's thought to amplify energy and combat negative thought patterns.

Sit and hold a piece, while thinking about what you want to achieve.

Daily Stress Busters

Monday
Shake your body, starting with your hands, then your arms, shoulders, torso, legs, ankles and feet.

Tuesday
Re-live the emotions of a time when you felt happy and secure.

Wednesday
Being an earth sign you love to get your fingers dirty so do some gardening, plant some seeds or repot your houseplants.

Thursday
Imagine you're laughing at something really funny. Feel the emotion spread from your stomach until the smile reaches your lips.

Friday
Switch your perspective and halt negative thoughts. Lay down and imagine the floor is the ceiling and vice versa.

Saturday
Connect with your earth element by laying on a patch of grass. Close your eyes and feel the springy blades between your fingers and toes.

Sunday
Get your practical head on and cook a new recipe for your friends and family.

Capricorn Self-love Ritual

Be kind and go easy on yourself with this gentle forgiveness ritual.

• Find a quiet outdoor spot, light a candle and get a piece of paper and a pen.

• Write down anything that is bothering you, including any guilt you feel for past mistakes.

• When you've finished, carefully pass the sheet of paper through the flame and toss it into a fireproof dish.

• Watch as it burns to ashes.

• To finish, empty the ashes into a bin, and say, 'I release the past, I release the pain, my heart is filled with love again.'

Daily Energizing Meditation

Picture yourself standing at the bottom of a mountain. It looms above you and when you look up, all you can see is glorious sunlight. The grass at your feet shimmers with new life and you can feel the energy bursting from each blade. You feel the urge to run, to let each springy shoot support you as you journey up the mountainside. You take a long, deep breath and draw it into your lungs, then you're off, shooting upwards, propelled by the warmth in your chest. You cannot see anything; all you can do is feel each deep breath. Finally, with super-human speed, you reach the top. The air is sweet and fresh as you inhale and exhale. You are bristling with energy.

Rejuvenating Rosemary for Capricorn

Rosemary is the ideal choice for hardworking goats, who need stamina, strength and focus. The refreshing scent enlivens the senses and brings you back to the present, boosting the immune system, circulation and memory.

To make a rejuvenating rosemary room spray, fill a small spray bottle three-quarters full of water. Add five drops of rosemary essential oil and two drops of orange essential oil. Seal the lid and give it a gentle shake to blend the scents. Spray around your home or office for vitality and inspiration!

Mindful Moment of Peace

Take a step back to alleviate stress and find inner peace.

Stop what you are doing. Bring your attention to your breath. As you inhale, imagine dropping back in your body; if it helps, take a physical step back. See your eyes as windows to the world and imagine you are peering through them, taking in the view. As you exhale, let go of any tension. Feel it slipping from your body. Each time you inhale, fall back a little further, and as you release the outward breath, release the stress. After a couple of minutes, you should feel a sense of stillness and distance from what is going on around you. You might even have filtered out external sounds, as you continue to focus on each breath.

A Good Night's Sleep

Sleep is just another activity on your list and you approach it methodically, going to bed and rising at the same time. While this helps your slumber patterns, overthinking can keep you awake. Try this sleep ritual to slow everything down.

• Lay down and place one hand on your belly. Take a long, slow breath in through the nose, and feel your hand rise gradually.

• Hold the breath for two or three counts, then exhale through your mouth and make a 'swooshing' noise as you do this.

• Continue for at least another ten breaths, paying attention to the rise of your hand and holding the breath before 'swooshing' as you exhale.

• For your last couple of breaths, hold the breath for an extra count and slow the rise and fall of the hand on your stomach.

Aquarius

20 January–18 February

Element
Air

Planet
Uranus

Aquarius Stars
Harry Styles (1 February)
Shakira (2 February)
Yoko Ono (18 February)

Mantra
'It is okay to pause and be still.'

The Essence of Aquarius

Adventurous and quirky, that's you, Aquarius. You dare to be different. Being a natural trailblazer, you follow your own unique path. It's all about what's new, from the latest technology to newly emerging philosophies; you love to learn and experience life and enjoy throwing yourself in at the deep end. If someone puts restrictions in your way, you'll go all out to prove them wrong. Intelligent and flexible, you need constant stimulation otherwise you become bored and irritable. Frustrations easily bubble over into anger, and this affects you on a deeper level, causing mood swings. For a flighty air sign, you're quite emotional and need the freedom to express yourself. Given free rein, you're at your creative best and able to achieve great things!

Your Self-care Plan

You need a plan that's as inventive as your mindset. It must balance the adventurous with the practical and help you find moments of calm in between the two. You have lots of nervous energy, so the rituals here will help you detach from the chaos and calm your emotions. They also work on building self-love into your routine. These techniques complement your love of the eccentric, but also help you switch off when you need to be in the moment.

Morning Ritual to Get Up and Glow

• Stand with your shoulders back, feet hip-width apart and weight equally balanced between each leg. Take a deep breath in and feel the stretch along your spine.

• As you exhale, picture a blazing sun, high in the sky. This symbolizes the positive energy of all the things you want to achieve.

Crystal Prescription

Your Aquarian mind easily takes flight and you're always on the lookout for new directions to explore. This sense of adventure makes every day a roller coaster. You love it, but it can increase stress. Your ideal choices are stones that balance the emotions without dampening your spirit.

Garnet

The stone of hope, garnet responds to your mood and balances the emotions, giving you the pick-me-up or calm you need.

Hold while breathing deeply, picturing yourself cloaked in the deep comforting hue.

Jade

Jade is the perfect choice to put busy Aquarians into a relaxed state of mind while inspiring creativity and balancing work and play.

Position a piece somewhere prominent in your living space to promote positive energy.

Daily Stress Busters

Monday
Tap into your air element. Go outside for a brisk walk. Run, jump and spin around with your arms outstretched. Notice the sensation of the air against your skin.

Tuesday
Soothe and revitalize your system by sipping a glass of warm water with some lemon slices.

Wednesday
On a clear night, go outside and look at the patterns of the stars. Identify constellations and take in the awesomeness of the universe.

Thursday
Quirky Aquarians tend to collect things. Spend ten minutes tidying your desk or closet and clear out what you don't need.

Friday
Listen to a new piece of music that you would not normally play. Close your eyes, and let the sounds create pictures in your mind.

Saturday
Switch off technology for a day and let the outside world be your stimulus.

Sunday
Add a couple of drops of juniper oil to a small bowl of hot water and inhale the uplifting aroma.

Aquarius Self-love Ritual

Don't lock yourself away when you're feeling low, feel the love and take yourself on a date!

• Make a list of what you'd really like to do, anything from a pampering bath to a trip to your favourite café for coffee and cake.

• Schedule at least one such activity each week as your date night and tick them off your list.

• If you make excuses, remind yourself, 'I deserve this!'

Daily Creative Meditation

Wherever you are, stop and close your eyes. Expand your attention so that you can see beyond your immediate surroundings. Breathe deeply and stretch your imagination even further and higher. Feel your attention float up and out until you have a bird's eye view and can see a vast expanse of land. Climb higher with every breath. When you're ready, return to the here and now. Feel your feet firmly on the ground providing balance and support.

Relaxing Lavender for Aquarius

Lavender has a lovely light scent which is often used to relax the muscles, induce calm and combat insomnia. It's the perfect choice for Aquarians, who often suffer with frayed nerves.

To make a lavender pillow, sew together two small squares of fabric, leaving a small opening. Roll a piece of paper into a makeshift funnel, then use it to fill the pillow with fragrant lavender flower heads before sewing up the opening. Pop it next to your pillow for a restful night's sleep.

Mindful Moment of Calm

Calm your emotions and find a moment of peace.

Place both hands on your midriff, just above your belly button. Take a long breath in through your nose, and then release this through your mouth. Take your time and steady the rhythm of your breathing. Feel the warmth beneath your fingers and focus on the rise and fall of your stomach. Picture a soothing pink light pouring from each palm. Inhale to fill your chest with loving energy; exhale to fill the rest of your body, helping you to relax. Continue to focus on breathing in the comforting pink energy for a couple of minutes.

A Good Night's Sleep

As a forward-thinking Aquarian, it's likely you'll be dreaming about your next big discovery. You might not want to switch off but clearing your mind of clutter is the best way to ensure a good night's rest.

• Imagine your headspace is a cave filled with thoughts, ideas and plans.

• As you breathe, you see an opening in the cave wall.

• For every outward breath, imagine throwing all those thoughts out through the opening.

• See them as sheets of paper being carried off by the wind.

• Continue to let them drift away on the breeze with every deep exhalation.

• Finally, enjoy the peace and silence of the cavernous space as you drift off to sleep.

Pisces

19 February–20 March

Element
Water

Planet
Neptune

Pisces Stars
Nina Simone (21 February)
Daniel Craig (2 March)
Lily Collins (18 March)

Mantra
'I embrace each new adventure.'

The Essence of Pisces

You are a creative powerhouse, Pisces, and one of the most imaginative zodiac signs. Your head is full of fancy, and then some, but that doesn't mean you can't be serious. You're a highly intuitive visionary, instinctively knowing what is right for you and others. This sixth sense makes you the go-to agony aunt for loved ones but while you love to be of service, you're deeply impressionable, and can sense pain from a mile away. It's hard for you to distance yourself emotionally, and this can dampen your spirits. Luckily for you, you get some respite from your playfulness and child-like sense of wonder. The key to your happiness is letting others in. With your whimsical ways, you're always going to be a winner.

Your Self-care Plan

Your plan needs to allow your sense of wonder to shine through, but also provide you with some key pointers so that you stay grounded and in control. These rituals encourage you to unleash your imagination and use it in a positive way to feel happy, fulfilled and connected with the environment. Exercises promote focus and clarity while honing your intuitive side.

Morning Ritual to Get Up and Glow

• Lie on your stomach with your arms alongside your body, palms up.

• Take a deep breath in, and lift your head, upper body, arms and legs off the floor, holding with your core muscles.

• If you can, hold for 30 seconds before relaxing. If you feel a strain in your neck, just lift your legs and upper body alternately.

• Repeat five times and extend the length of the hold for another ten seconds, if it is comfortable to do so.

Crystal Prescription

You easily absorb other people's emotions. While this makes you a great friend and counsellor, it can also induce low moods when you feel vulnerable and overwhelmed. You need crystals to protect you from external stress and keep you strong and centred.

Hematite

Glossy and gorgeous, this stone will help you shine. It has a grounding energy, which acts like a protective shield and promotes strength and positivity.

Hold in both hands and picture yourself cocooned in a dome of light.

Aquamarine

This beautiful stone is associated with the element of water. It balances the emotions and calms the mind so it will help you release pain and fear and move forward with confidence.

Place beside your bath, and meditate on the colour of the stone as you soak.

Daily Stress Busters

Monday
Get close to your water element – take a walk by a river, paddle in the sea or go for a swim.

Tuesday
Wrap an ice cube in a soft cloth, then roll it over your forehead and the back of your neck.

Wednesday
Burn some uplifting geranium essential oil or add a few drops to your bath water.

Thursday
Drink a long glass of water and focus solely on the way it smells, feels and tastes.

Friday
Find a picture you really like and imagine stepping into it. Let your mind wander and enjoy the daydream.

Saturday
Sit in your local park with a notebook and write about something you see.

Sunday
Think about where you'd like to be in five years' time. See, feel and experience the future as you'd like it to be.

Pisces Self-love Ritual

You're one of the most romantic signs of the zodiac, but you need to focus on yourself instead of always focusing on others.

• Find a photograph of yourself that you like and look at it.

• Imagine the person is someone you know and write a poem or a description to capture their beauty.

• Focus on the things you love about the picture and any emotions it stirs.

• Keep the poem and read it every so often as a reminder of your inner and outer beauty.

Daily Stimulating Meditation

You are standing beneath a sparkling waterfall. All around you, tiny droplets of water tumble, cascading down the mountainside, carving a path into the rock. From your vantage point you are cloaked beneath the falling water, able to watch it flow but still remain dry. You realize it is time to experience this phenomenon for yourself. Take a deep breath in and, as you exhale, move into the flow. Icy fingers brush your head as the water covers you. Soothing and energizing, the shower falls, and you stand at the centre. Your heart is pumping, your lungs drink in the fresh air. You feel alive and ready for anything!

Magical Lemon Balm for Pisces

You are naturally intuitive, but you can build on this power and boost your vitality using lemon balm, an invigorating herb that lifts the mood and also soothes the stomach, while promoting a sense of relaxation

To make a magical lemon balm tincture, chop a few handfuls of lemon balm and put in a small jar, then cover to the top with vodka. Seal the jar and store in a cool, dark place for six weeks. Strain the liquid into a dropper bottle. Take up to five drops to relax and help you tune into your intuition.

Mindful Moment of Balance

Restore balance and bring yourself back to the moment by connecting with the elements.

Stand outside quietly and absorb the atmosphere. Engage all your senses and consider what you can see. How does the landscape look and how is it affected by the weather? If it's raining, it might appear fresh and vivid. If it's sunny you might notice a lovely blue sky. Next, consider what you can hear. Is the wind rushing through the trees or can you hear the gentle patter of raindrops? How does everything smell and feel? Notice your mood, and the way you are breathing. Engage with the weather and enjoy connecting with the elements.

A Good Night's Sleep

Sleep is not just restorative to the dreamy Piscean, it's a whole new realm to explore. You dream most nights, and probably receive insights while you doze. Eight hours isn't enough, and if it weren't for your daily adventures, you'd happily stay in bed. With you it's all about the quality of sleep, so a ritual that brings on deep relaxation is key.

• Lay down and make sure you are comfortable.

• Breathe deeply and close your eyes.

• Think of a serene setting, a place where you feel calm and at peace. This could be a real or imaginary location.

• Picture yourself there and engage your senses. What can you see, hear, smell, taste, touch?

• Take a moment to enjoy being in this space.

• Breathe in the peace and breathe out any tension.

Tune into Your Cosmic Energy

The hints, tips and rituals in this book are tailored to each star sign and based on the characteristics and strengths they possess. They are designed to help you every day, whether you need to de-stress, get into the creative zone or boost energy levels.

Once you have read your own zodiac sign, remember that while you might be typical to your sign in many ways, you are also unique, so don't limit yourself to one chapter in the book. Engage your imagination and think about the qualities you need in any given situation, then use the table opposite to lead you to a ritual that will help you absorb that energy. Go with what feels right for you. Practical Capricorn could develop leadership skills from front-runner Aries; solid Taurus can impart determination to mercurial Gemini.

Get your thinking-cap on and create your own self-care plan by mixing and matching rituals or be inventive and come up with your own ideas based on the suggestions. Use the power of the signs of the zodiac to help you identify skills and latent talents.

Here's a quick guide to your sign's cosmic energy, to help you live your best life.

Zodiac sign	Energy	Planet
Aries	Activity	Mars
Taurus	Tenacity	Venus
Gemini	Creativity	Mercury
Cancer	Sensitivity	Moon
Leo	Boldness	Sun
Virgo	Practicality	Mercury
Libra	Balance	Venus
Scorpio	Power	Mars
Sagittarius	Independence	Jupiter
Capricorn	Stability	Saturn
Aquarius	Inventiveness	Uranus
Pisces	Imagination	Neptune

Tune into the vibrations of your cosmic energy and use these rituals to learn to live your best life.

MANAGING DIRECTOR
Sarah Lavelle

COMMISSIONING EDITOR
Stacey Cleworth

EDITORIAL ASSISTANT
Sofie Shearman

SENIOR DESIGNER
Katherine Keeble

ILLUSTRATOR
Eleanor Hardiman

HEAD OF PRODUCTION
Stephen Lang

PRODUCTION CONTROLLER
Sabeena Atchia

Safety note

The herbal remedies in this book are not a replacement for professional health advice. Herbal medicine is vast and complex and must be used responsibly. Many herbal products, including essential oils, are not recommended for people who are pregnant, nursing, have allergies, a medical condition, or taking medications, due to their high potency. Consult your healthcare professional prior to use if you have any concerns or questions.

Published in 2022 by Quadrille, an imprint of Hardie Grant Publishing

Quadrille
52–54 Southwark Street
London SE1 1UN
quadrille.com

Text © Alison Davies 2022
Illustrations © Eleanor Hardiman 2022
Compilation, design and layout © Quadrille 2022

Cataloguing in Publication Data: a catalogue record for this book is available from the British Library.

ISBN 978 1 78713 813 1

Reprinted in 2022
10 9 8 7 6 5 4 3 2

Printed in China

MIX
Paper from
responsible sources
FSC™ C020056